Table of Contents

A heart attack occurs when the flow of blood to the heart is severely reduced or blocked. The blockage is usually due to a buildup of fat, cholesterol and other substances in the heart (coronary) arteries. The fatty, cholesterol-containing deposits are called plaques. The process of plaque buildup is called atherosclerosis.

Sometimes, a plaque can rupture and form a clot that blocks blood flow. A lack of blood flow can damage or destroy part of the heart muscle.

A heart attack is also called a myocardial infarction.

Prompt treatment is needed for a heart attack to prevent death. Call emergency medical help if you think you might be having a heart attack.

BREAKFAST

1. Egg Pepper Rings with Carrot Salsa

Prep Time: 20 Minutes

Cook Time: 25 Minutes

Servings: 4

Ingredients

- 1 each medium red and yellow pepper
- 2 tbsp. Extra virgin olive oil
- 2 large carrots, coarsely grated
- 1 pint cherry or grape tomatoes, quartered
- 1 clove garlic, finely chopped
- 1/2 c. fresh cilantro, roughly chopped
- 8 large eggs
- 1/2 tsp. dried oregano
- Salt and pepper
- Toasted English Muffins (optional)

Instructions

1. Slice the peppers into eight 1/2-inch-thick rings. Dice the remaining peppers and transfer to a medium bowl.

2. Heat 1 tablespoon oil in a large nonstick skillet over medium heat. Add the pepper rings and cook until they begin to soften and turn golden brown, 3 to 4 minutes per side.

3. Meanwhile, in a bowl, toss the diced peppers, carrots, tomatoes and garlic with the remaining tablespoon oil and a pinch each salt and pepper, then fold in the cilantro.

4. Crack 1 egg into each pepper ring; sprinkle with oregano and 1/4 teaspoon each salt and pepper. Cover and cook until the whites are set, 4 to 5 minutes for soft yolks. Top with the carrot salsa and serve on English muffins (if using).

Prep Time: 20 Minutes

Cook Time: 15 Minutes

Servings: 12

Ingredients

- 2 tbsp. butter
- 1 medium onion
- 2 tsp. Fresh parsley
- 1 tsp. fresh basil
- 1/2 c. mushrooms
- 10 oz. frozen chopped spinach
- 6 large eggs
- 1/4 c. milk
- 6 oz. feta cheese
- 1/4 tsp. salt
- tsp. Pepper
- 9 unbaked deep-dish piecrust
- 2 tsp. Grated Parmesan cheese

Instructions

1. Preheat oven to 375 degrees F. Melt butter in skillet over medium heat. Add onion, parsley, basil and mushrooms; cook, stirring occasionally, for 4 to 5 minutes, until softened. Remove from heat. Squeeze excess liquid from thawed spinach; add to onion mixture and stir.

2. In bowl, whisk together eggs and next four ingredients; stir in spinach mixture. Pour into piecrust and spread evenly. Sprinkle Parmesan evenly over top. Bake for 30 minutes, until puffed and lightly browned and center is set. Serve with sliced tomatoes and toast.

Prep Time: 20 Minutes

Cook Time: 15 Minutes

Servings: 8

Ingredients

- 6 slice bacon
- 2 tbsp. Dijon mustard with seeds
- 12 slice firm white bread
- 1 1/2 c. shredded Gruyère cheese
- 9 large eggs
- 3 c. whole milk
- 1/2 tsp. salt
- 1/4 tsp. Freshly ground black pepper

Instructions

1. Lay bacon on paper towels, folded double thick, on a microwave-safe plate, and cover with a single paper towel. Microwave on high, 2 to 3 minutes, or until browned. Let stand 5 minutes, or until cool and crisp. Crumble bacon coarsely.

2. Grease 9" x 13" ceramic or glass baking dish.

3. Spread mustard on 1 side of each bread slice. Arrange 6 slices, mustard side up, in baking dish, cutting them to fit if necessary. Sprinkle with half of cheese. Top with all but 2 Tbsp. crumbled bacon, then remaining bread slices, mustard side up.

4. Beat eggs, milk, salt and pepper in a large bowl with a wire whisk until blended. Slowly pour egg mixture all over bread slices; press bread down to help it absorb eggs. If necessary, spoon egg mixture over any uncoated bread. Sprinkle with remaining cheese and bacon. Let stand at room temperature 15 minutes, or cover and refrigerate overnight.

5. Preheat oven to 350°F. Bake strata 40 minutes, or until puffed and golden and knife inserted in center comes out clean. Let stand at least 10 minutes before serving.

Prep Time: 25 Minutes

Cook Time: 30 Minutes

Servings: 4

Ingredients

- 1/4 c. chopped red onion
- 2 medium ripe tomatoes
- 1/4 c. loosley packed fresh cilantro leaves
- 4 large eggs
- 4 large egg whites
- Salt and pepper
- 1 c. fat-free refried beans
- 1/4 tsp. ground chipotle chile
- 4 Whole wheat tortillas

Instructions

1. Prepare salsa: In cup of ice water, soak chopped onion 10 minutes; drain well. In small bowl, combine onion, tomato, and cilantro; set aside.

2. In medium bowl, with wire whisk or fork, beat whole eggs, egg whites, 1/8 teaspoon salt, and 1/8 teaspoon freshly ground black pepper until blended.

3. Spray 10-inch nonstick skillet with cooking spray; heat on medium 1 minute. Pour egg mixture into skillet; cook about 5 minutes or until egg mixture is set but still moist, stirring occasionally.

4. Meanwhile, in microwave-safe small bowl, mix beans and chipotle chile. Cover with vented plastic wrap; heat in microwave on High 1 minute or until hot.

5. Place stack of tortillas between damp paper towels on microwave-safe plate; heat in microwave on High 10 to 15 seconds to warm. To serve, layer each tortilla with eggs, beans, and salsa.

Prep Time: 30 Minutes

Cook Time: 2hrs 30 Minutes

Servings: 1

Ingredients

- 1/2 c. milk
- 2 tbsp. milk
- 1 package active dry yeast
- 3 c. all-purpose flour
- 1/4 c. granulated sugar
- 1 tsp. kosher salt
- 1/4 c. unsalted butter
- 1/4 c. unsalted butter
- 1 tbsp. unsalted butter
- vegetable oil
- 1/4 c. packed light brown sugar
- 1 tsp. ground cinnamon
- 1 c. confectioners' sugar
- 1 tsp. pure vanilla extract

Instructions

1. In a small saucepan, heat 1/2 cup milk and 1/2 cup water on medium-low heat until warm but not hot to touch.

2. Meanwhile, in a large bowl, whisk together the yeast, 1 cup flour, and 2 tablespoons granulated sugar. Stir in the warm milk mixture. Cover and set aside until thick and foamy, about 15 minutes.

3. Mix in the salt and 1/4 cup melted butter. Gradually mix in the remaining 2 cups flour. Cover and let rise until doubled in size, about 1 hour.

4. Meanwhile, lightly coat a 9- by 13-inch pan with oil. Line the pan with parchment, leaving a 3-inch overhang on the 2 long sides; coat the parchment. In a small bowl, combine the brown sugar, cinnamon, and the remaining 2 tablespoons granulated sugar.

5. Punch down the dough. Turn out onto a floured surface and knead until it comes together. Roll into a 9- by 12-inch rectangle. Spread with the 1/4 cup softened butter and sprinkle with the cinnamon-sugar mixture. Starting from the long side, roll the dough into a tight log, pinching the seam to seal.

6. Slide a long piece of unflavored dental floss under the log of dough about 1 inch from the end. Holding the

thread taut, lift the ends and cross to cut off a piece of dough. Repeat to cut twelve 1-inch-thick rolls. Transfer the rolls cut-side up to the prepared pan, spacing them equally. Cover and let rise until the rolls are touching, about 20 minutes.

7. Meanwhile, heat the oven to 375 degrees F. Bake the rolls until puffed and lightly golden brown, 25 to 27 minutes.

8. During the last 5 minutes of cooking, in a small saucepan, whisk together the confectioners' sugar, vanilla, remaining 2 tablespoons milk, and remaining 1 tablespoon butter and cook over low heat until smooth, 2 minutes. Drizzle over the cinnamon rolls.

Prep Time: 30 Minutes

Cook Time: 2hrs 35 Minutes

Servings: 8

Ingredients

Dough:

- 2 1/2 c. all-purpose flour
- 1/4 c. granulated sugar
- 1 package active dry yeast (about 2 1/4 teaspoons total)
- 1/2 tsp. kosher salt
- 1/4 c. whole milk
- 4 tbsp. unsalted butter
- 3 large eggs
- 1 tsp. pure vanilla extract

Filling:

- 1/4 c. packed brown sugar
- 1 tsp. ground cinnamon
- 1/4 tsp. freshly grated nutmeg
- 4 tbsp. unslated butter

- 1 Golden Delicious apple

- Caramel sauce and coarse salt

Instructions

1. In a large bowl (or the bowl of an electric mixer), whisk together the flour, sugar, yeast, and salt. Place the milk and butter in a small heavy-bottomed saucepan and cook over low heat until the butter melts, 5 to 6 minutes. Remove from heat.

2. Add the milk mixture to the flour mixture, then add the eggs and vanilla. With the mixer on low, beat until the flour mixture is moistened. Increase the speed to medium and mix until the dough is smooth, about 6 minutes. Scrape the dough down in the bowl to loosen it, then cover with plastic wrap and a dishtowel. Set the bowl in a warm place and let the dough rise until it doubles in size, about 45 minutes.

3. While the dough is rising, line a 4 1/2- by 8 1/2-inch loaf pan with parchment paper, leaving a 3-inch overhang on the long sides. Butter the parchment and the sides of the pan. In a small bowl, combine the brown sugar, cinnamon, and nutmeg. In a microwave-safe bowl, melt the butter.

4. Punch the dough down, then transfer to a lightly floured work surface and roll into a 12- by 18-inch rectangle. If the dough is sticking, sprinkle the underside with a bit more flour. Arrange the dough so the long side is in front of you. Brush the melted butter over the dough, then sprinkle with the brown sugar mixture.

5. Core and cut the apple into 1/4-inch pieces. Cut the dough crosswise into 6 even strips. Sprinkle 1 strip with some of the apples, gently pressing them into the dough. Top with another strip of dough and more apples; repeat with the remaining strips of dough and apples. Cut the stack into 6 equal portions. Stand the prepared loaf pan on one of its short sides, and arrange the stacks with cut sides facing out (tucking in any fallen apples). Cover and let rise for 20 minutes.

6. Heat oven to 350 degrees F. Bake the loaf until deep golden brown, 40 to 45 minutes. Let cool in the pan for 5 minutes, then transfer to a wire rack and let cool for 10 minutes more. Drizzle with caramel sauce and sprinkle with coarse salt, if desired.

Prep Time: 25 Minutes

Cook Time: 1hrs 25 Minutes

Servings: 6

Ingredients

- 1/4 c. olive oil
- 3 tbsp. olive oil
- 1 medium Yellow Onion
- 1 1/2 tsp. salt
- 1 1/2 lb. red potatoes
- 1/2 tsp. Freshly ground pepper
- 8 large eggs
- 1/2 c. chopped green olives
- 1/4 lb. aged Manchego cheese

Instructions

1. Preheat oven to 350 degrees F. In a 10- or 12-inch ovenproof nonstick skillet over medium heat, heat 2 tablespoons oil. Add onion and 1/2 teaspoon salt, and cook, stirring occasionally, until onion is soft and

translucent, 8 to 10 minutes. Transfer onion to a large bowl and set aside.

2. In the same skillet over medium heat, heat 2 tablespoons oil. Working in batches, add half of potatoes in an even layer and season with 1/2 teaspoon salt and 1/4 teaspoon pepper. Cook, stirring occasionally, until potatoes begin to soften, 8 to 10 minutes.

3. Add eggs and olives to reserved onion-potato mixture, and gently stir to combine.

4. Wipe the skillet clean. Over medium heat, heat remaining olive oil. Add half of reserved potato-onion-egg mixture to skillet, smoothing with the back of a spoon to create an even layer. Top with cheese; then cover with remaining potato mixture, smoothing with the back of a spoon to create an even layer. Cook for 10 minutes on stovetop, then transfer skillet to oven.

5. Bake until eggs are set and potatoes are tender, 25 to 30 minutes. Adjust oven to broil and cook tortilla until top is lightly browned, about 3 minutes. Transfer pan to a wire rack and let cool for 5 minutes. Invert onto a serving plate and cut into 6 or 12 wedges. Serve hot or at room temperature.

Prep Time: 35 Minutes

Cook Time: 50 Minutes

Servings: 6

Ingredients

- 8 oz. Asparagus
- 6 oz. shiitake mushrooms
- 1/4 c. olive oil
- 2 clove garlic
- Salt
- Pepper
- 1 1/2 lb. pizza dough
- 5 slice bacon
- 6 oz. Fontina cheese
- 6 large eggs

Instructions

1. Arrange oven racks in top and bottom thirds of oven. Preheat oven to 475 degrees F. Lightly grease two 18-inch by 12-inch jelly-roll pans.

2. Slice asparagus on an angle into 2-inch pieces. Transfer to large bowl, along with mushrooms, oil, garlic, and 1/4 teaspoon salt; toss until well coated.

3. Divide dough into 6 balls. On lightly floured surface, with floured rolling pin, roll and press 1 dough ball into 6-inch round; place on prepared pan. Repeat with remaining dough.

4. Evenly divide asparagus mixture among rounds, creating well in center of each. Bake 10 minutes or until edges are golden brown, switching pans halfway through.

5. Meanwhile, place bacon on paper-towel-lined plate. Cover with 2 sheets paper towel. Microwave on High 4 to 6 minutes or until beginning to crisp. Cool slightly; tear bacon into small pieces.

6. Sprinkle pizzettes with bacon and Fontina. Bake 1 to 2 minutes or until cheese melts. Carefully crack eggs directly onto centers of pizzettes. Bake 6 to 8 minutes or until whites are opaque and set, switching pans halfway through. Sprinkle with pepper and salt; serve warm.

Prep Time: 15 Minutes

Cook Time: 35 Minutes

Servings: 4

Ingredients

- 4 slice Italian bread
- 1 medium zucchini
- 1 clove garlic
- 1 tbsp. olive oil
- 4 ripe plum tomatoes
- Salt and pepper
- 1 c. part-skim ricotta cheese
- 1/4 c. freshly grated Pecorino Romano cheese
- 4 oz. fresh mozzarella cheese

Instructions

1. Preheat toaster oven to 450 degrees F. Toast bread 5 to 10 minutes or until golden.
2. In microwave-safe medium bowl, combine zucchini, garlic, and oil. Microwave on High 4 minutes, stirring

once. Add tomatoes, 1/4 teaspoon salt, and 1/4 teaspoon freshly ground black pepper; cover with vented plastic wrap and microwave on High 3 minutes.

3. Meanwhile, thinly slice basil leaves; reserve 2 tablespoons for garnish. In small bowl, combine basil, ricotta, Romano, 1/8 teaspoon salt, and 1/4 teaspoon freshly ground black pepper.

4. Spread one-fourth of ricotta mixture on each bread slice. Using slotted spoon, divide tomato mixture evenly among bread slices; top with mozzarella.

5. In single layer on foil-lined toaster oven tray (working in batches if necessary), bake toasts 8 to 10 minutes or until heated through and mozzarella is melted and lightly browned. Garnish with reserved basil.

Prep Time: 1hrs 15 Minutes

Cook Time: 2hrs 45 Minutes

Servings: 40

Ingredients

- 1 1/2 c. whole milk
- 3/4 tsp. kosher salt
- 1 1/2 c. coarse or stone-ground grits
- 1/2 c. heavy cream
- 6 oz. country ham
- 6 oz. Thomasville Tomme cheese or Gouda
- 6 c. canola or peanut oil
- c. all-purpose flour

Instructions

1. In a medium saucepan over high heat, bring 2 cups water, milk, and 3/4 teaspoon salt to a boil. Reduce heat to medium and slowly add grits in a stream, whisking constantly to avoid lumps.

2. Reduce heat to low and add heavy cream. Cook over low heat, stirring frequently, until grits are completely soft, about 50 to 60 minutes. Remove from heat, stir ham into grits, and let grits cool completely. (Grits can be cooked up to a day ahead and stored, covered, in refrigerator.)

3. Using a small ice-cream scoop or a spoon, scoop up about 2 teaspoons grits. Insert a cube of cheese into grits and, using your hands, shape grits around cheese to form a ball. Repeat with remaining grits and cheese.

4. Heat oil to 350 degrees F in a large pot fitted with a deep-fry thermometer over medium-high heat. Preheat oven to 250 degrees F. Place flour on a small plate. In batches of 6, roll fritters in flour to lightly coat, then deep-fry until golden brown, 2 to 3 minutes. Transfer fritters to paper towels to drain. Season with salt, then transfer to a sheet pan in oven to keep warm until all batches have been fried.

11. Spicy Orange and Sesame Chicken Sandwiches

Prep Time: 15 Minutes

Cook Time: 45 Minutes

Servings: 6

Ingredients

- 1 1/2 lb. Boneless Chicken Breasts
- 3/4 tsp. salt
- 1/2 tsp. black pepper
- 2 tbsp. butter
- 1/2 c. orange marmalade
- 2 1/2 tbsp. Sesame Oil
- 2 1/2 tbsp. Soy Sauce
- 3/4 tsp. hot sauce
- 1/2 tsp. cayenne pepper
- 1/2 tsp. sesame seeds
- 2 medium oranges
- 1 small head of butter lettuce
- 3 large pocket-style pitas

Instructions

1. Heat oven to 400 degrees F.

2. Season the chicken on all sides with the salt and pepper and place in a baking dish. Dot the top of the skin with the butter and place in the oven on the center rack. Roast for 10 minutes.

3. Mix the marmalade, sesame oil, soy sauce, hot sauce, and cayenne pepper together in a small bowl and use it to baste the chicken frequently until the meat reaches 167 degrees F -- about 20 more minutes.

4. Adjust oven to broil, sprinkle the sesame seeds over the chicken and broil until seeds are toasted and skin is crispy -- about 1 minute.

5. Remove the breasts from the oven and let rest for 15 minutes.

6. Bring the basting sauce to a boil and cook for 1 minute. Remove from the heat and let cool.

7. Cut the skin and pith from the oranges and slice into 1/4-inch-thick rounds. Remove any seeds.

8. Slice the chicken and place equal amounts of it, the oranges, and lettuce leaves inside the pitas. Drizzle each sandwich with the boiled sauce.

Prep Time: 1hrs Minutes

Cook Time: 1hrs 20 Minutes

Servings: 4

Ingredients

- 4 large artichokes
- 3 tbsp. olive oil
- 2 medium carrot
- 2 clove garlic
- 1/4 c. fresh mint
- 3 tbsp. Fresh parsley
- 1 c. couscous
- 1 1/2 c. chicken broth
- 1/2 tsp. salt
- 1/4 tsp. coarsely ground black pepper
- 1 lemon
- Parsley sprigs for garnish

Instructions

1. Prepare and cook artichokes.

2. Meanwhile, preheat oven to 400 degrees F. In nonstick 10-inch skillet, heat 1 tablespoon olive oil over medium heat. Add carrots and cook until tender, about 10 minutes. Stir in garlic, cook 1 minute longer. Remove to medium bowl. Dice artichoke stems, add to carrot mixture with mint and parsley.

3. Prepare couscous as label directs but use 1 cup chicken broth in place of water. When couscous is done, stir in salt, pepper, carrot mixture, and remaining 2 tablespoons olive oil.

4. Pour remaining 1/2 cup chicken broth into shallow baking dish large enough to hold all artichokes (about 13" by 9"), arrange artichokes in dish. Spoon couscous mixture between artichoke leaves and into center cavities. Bake 15 to 20 minutes until artichokes are heated through. Serve artichokes with lemon wedges and garnish with parsley sprigs.

5. Each main-dish serving: About 350 calories, 11 g protein, 54 g carbohydrate, 11 g total fat (2 g saturated), 4 mg cholesterol, 600 mg sodium.

Prep Time: 15 Minutes

Cook Time: 20 Minutes

Servings: 2

Ingredients

- 16 medium shrimp
- 3 tsp. fresh lime juice
- 1/4 c. Extra virgin olive oil
- 1/2 tsp. Sea salt
- 1/4 tsp. crushed red pepper
- 1 large pink grapefruit
- 1 tsp. Dijon mustard
- 1 head butter lettuce
- 1/2 c. arugula
- 1 avocado

Instructions

1. Grill the shrimp. Heat a grill to medium. Toss the shrimp with 2 teaspoons lime juice, 1 tablespoon olive oil, 1/4 teaspoon salt, and red pepper. Marinate for 15

minutes. Thread shrimp onto skewers; grill until pink and cooked through -- about 1 minute each side. Set aside and keep warm.

2. Assemble the salad. Cut the peel from the grapefruit using a sharp knife. Cut out the segments, reserving the juice. Squeeze the juice from the remaining pith and pulp. Strain and measure 3 tablespoons juice. Set remaining juice aside for another use.

3. Whisk the Dijon, remaining 1/4 teaspoon salt, remaining 1 teaspoon lime juice, and the reserved grapefruit juice together. Whisk in remaining 3 tablespoons olive oil. Line 2 salad plates with lettuce and arugula. Arrange the shrimp, grapefruit, and avocado on top of the greens. Drizzle with grapefruit vinaigrette. Serve immediately.

Prep Time: 10 Minutes

Cook Time: 15 Minutes

Servings: 4

Ingredients

- 8 slice thick-cut smoked bacon
- 1 package button mushrooms
- 1 medium Red Onion
- 4 large eggs
- 2 1/2 tbsp. red wine vinegar
- 1 tbsp. extra-virgin olive oil
- 1 1/2 tsp. honey Dijon mustard
- 1/2 tsp. kosher salt
- 12 c. baby spinach
- 12 oz. mixed cherry tomatoes

Instructions

1. In a large skillet, cook bacon over medium heat until crisp. Remove from pan with a slotted spoon; drain on a paper towel. Reserve 3 tablespoon of bacon

drippings; discard remainder. Break up bacon into bite-size pieces when bacon is cool enough to handle.

2. Heat 1 1/2 tablespoons of bacon drippings in the same skillet over medium-high heat. Add mushrooms and cook 4 to 6 minutes, stirring frequently, until lightly browned. Add onion; cook 1 to 2 minutes, stirring frequently. Transfer mixture to a large mixing bowl.

3. Make poached eggs: Fill a large saucepan with 3 inches of water. Add 1 tablespoon white vinegar (this helps whites coagulate). Bring to a gentle simmer. Crack each egg into a small cup, then slide eggs, one at a time, into water. Cook 5 to 7 minutes, adjusting heat accordingly to keep at a gentle simmer, until whites are set and yolks are slightly runny. Poach longer if you like firmer yolks.

4. Remove eggs with a slotted spoon. Transfer eggs to a paper towel.

5. In same skillet over medium heat, whisk red wine vinegar, remaining 1 1/2 tablespoons bacon drippings, olive oil, mustard, and salt until well blended and warmed-through. Add spinach to mushroom mixture in bowl and pour warm dressing over; toss to coat. Add tomatoes and reserved bacon pieces. Divide salad

into 4 servings. Top each with a poached egg; season with salt and freshly ground black pepper to taste.

Prep Time: 10 Minutes

Cook Time: 15 Minutes

Servings: 4

Ingredients

- 2 tbsp. extra-virgin olive oil
- 2 clove garlic cloves
- 1 lb. button or wild mushrooms (such as porcini, cremini, shiitake) with stems removed
- 1/4 c. white wine
- 1/2 tsp. salt
- 1/4 tsp. Freshly ground pepper
- 24 slice slices countrystyle bread (preferably ciabatta)
- 1 lb. fresh salted buffalo mozzarella
- 2 tbsp. chopped fresh Italian parsley

Instructions

1. Preheat oven to 375 degrees F. In a 12-inch nonstick skillet, heat olive oil over medium-high heat. Sauté garlic until fragrant, about 30 seconds. Add chopped

mushrooms and sauté 3 to 4 minutes. Pour in wine; increase heat to high and cook, stirring, until liquid evaporates, about 5 minutes. Mix in salt and pepper.

2. Arrange bread on a large country-style bread baking sheet. Top each piece with a slice of mozzarella. Bake 5 to 7 minutes, until cheese is melted.

3. Top crostini with mushroom mixture; sprinkle with parsley. Serve warm.

Prep Time: 15 Minutes

Cook Time: 3hrs 15 Minutes

Servings: 4

Ingredients

Slow-Cooked Chicken:

- 1 1/2 tsp. Italian herb seasoning
- 1 tsp. smoked paprika
- 1/2 tsp. kosher salt
- 1/2 tsp. Freshly ground pepper
- 6 chicken thighs without skin
- 1 tbsp. extra-virgin olive oil
- 1/2 c. dry white wine
- 4 clove garlic

Panini:

- 4 squares focaccia (about 1-inch thick)
- 1 jar roasted peppers (preferably red and yellow)
- 4 oz. sliced provolone cheese
- Olive oil cooking spray

Instructions

1. Slow-Cooked Chicken: Mix Italian seasoning, paprika, salt, and pepper in a small cup. Brush chicken with olive oil; rub seasoning mixture all over chicken. Put wine and garlic in a 4 1/2- to 6-quart slow-cooker; add chicken thighs in a single layer, bone side down. Cover; cook on low-heat setting for 4 hours, or until fork tender.

2. Remove from cooker; let stand until cool enough to handle (chicken can be cooked up to 1 day ahead and refrigerated). Remove bones; tear chicken into large pieces.

3. Panini: Assemble sandwiches on focaccia with chicken, roasted peppers, and provolone. Spray sandwiches with olive oil cooking spray. Grill sandwiches in a panini press or sandwich grill, or on a stovetop grill pan with a heavy skillet on top. Grill sandwiches until bread is lightly toasted and cheese is melted, about 5 minutes.

Prep Time: 15 Minutes

Cook Time: 35 Minutes

Servings: 1

Ingredients

- 4 c. water
- 4 c. chicken broth
- 2 tbsp. extra-virgin olive oil
- 2 tbsp. unsalted butter
- 1 c. onion
- 1/2 c. dry white wine
- 1 lb. large shrimp
- 3/4 lb. Asparagus
- 2 plum tomatoes
- 1/4 c. Parmesan cheese
- 1/4 c. basil leaves
- 3/4 tsp. salt
- Freshly ground black pepper
- shaved Parmesan cheese

Instructions

1. Heat 4 cups of the broth mixture in a saucepan over low heat. Refrigerate remaining broth mixture, up to 3 days, for finishing risotto.

2. In a deep nonstick skillet, heat 1 tablespoon each of the olive oil and butter over medium heat. Add onion; sauté 3 minutes. Add rice; cook and stir 2 minutes. Add wine; cook 2 minutes.

3. Add 1 cup of hot broth mixture and cook, stirring, until broth is absorbed. Continue adding broth, 1/2 cup at a time, until all is incorporated, about 15 minutes. The risotto will be very al dente. Remove from heat; pour risotto on a baking sheet and spread into a thin layer. Cool completely. Transfer to a food-storage bag; refrigerate up to 3 days.

4. Heat remaining broth mixture in a saucepan until hot. Heat the remaining 1 tablespoon each oil and butter in a deep nonstick skillet over medium-high heat; add shrimp and asparagus and sauté 2 minutes. Stir in partially cooked risotto and 1 cup hot broth. Cook, stirring, until broth is absorbed. Cook and stir 7 minutes longer, adding hot broth mixture 1/2 cup at a time, until risotto is creamy. Stir in tomatoes, grated cheese, basil, salt, and pepper. Spoon into shallow

bowls. Top each serving with shaved Parmesan cheese, if desired.

Prep Time: 15 Minutes

Cook Time: 35 Minutes

Servings: 4

Ingredients

- 1 large egg
- 1/3 c. panko
- 1 tsp. ground cumin
- 1/4 tsp. ground allspice
- 1/8 tsp. ground cinnamon
- Kosher salt and pepper
- 3 cloves garlic, divided
- 1 lb. ground beef
- 1 pint cherry tomatoes, halved
- 1 14.5-oz can chickpeas, rinsed
- 1 tbsp. olive oil
- 1/4 c. crumbled feta
- 1/4 c. cup fresh flat-leaf parsley, chopped
- Couscous, for serving

Instructions

1. Heat broiler. In a large bowl, beat egg, then add panko, spices, 1/2 tsp salt, and 1/4 tsp pepper. Finely grate in 2 cloves garlic. Mix in beef, then shape into 12 balls.

2. Transfer meatballs to a rimmed baking sheet, then broil on a rack in the upper portion of the oven until browned, 2 to 3 minutes. Reduce oven temperature to 425°F. Remove meatballs from oven and carefully pour out any excess fat.

3. In a bowl, toss tomatoes and chickpeas with oil, remaining clove garlic (thinly sliced), and 1/4 tsp each salt and pepper. Add to pan with meatballs and roast until tomatoes have softened, about 10 minutes. Remove from oven, top with feta and parsley, and serve with couscous.

Prep Time: 25 Minutes

Cook Time: 50 Minutes

Servings: 6

Ingredients

Minestrone:

- 1 c. pearl barley
- 1 tbsp. olive oil
- 2 c. green cabbage
- 2 large carrots
- 2 large celery stalks
- 1 medium onion
- 1 clove garlic
- 3 c. water
- 2 can vegetable broth
- 1 can diced tomatoes
- Salt
- 1 medium zucchini
- 1/2 lb. green beans

Light Pesto:

- 1 c. fresh basil leaves

- 2 tbsp. olive oil

- 2 tbsp. water

- salt

- 1/4 c. Romano CHeese

- 1 clove garlic

Instruction

1. Heat 5- to 6-quart Dutch oven over medium-high heat until hot. Add barley and cook 3 to 4 minutes or until toasted and fragrant, stirring constantly. Transfer barley to small bowl; set aside.

2. In same Dutch oven, heat oil over medium-high heat until hot. Add cabbage, carrots, celery, and onion; cook 8 to 10 minutes or until vegetables are tender and lightly browned, stirring occasionally. Add garlic and cook 30 seconds or until fragrant. Stir in barley, water, broth, tomatoes, and 1/4 teaspoon salt. Cover and heat to boiling over high heat. Reduce heat to low and simmer, covered, 25 minutes.

3. Stir zucchini and beans into barley mixture; increase heat to medium and cook, covered, 10 to 15 minutes longer or until all vegetables and barley are tender.

Nutritional information is based on 1 serving of soup without pesto

4. In blender container with narrow base or in mini food processor, combine basil, oil, water, and 1/4 teaspoon salt; cover and blend until mixture is pureed. Transfer pesto to small bowl; stir in Romano and garlic. Makes about 1/2 cup pesto.

5. Ladle minestrone into 6 large soup bowls. Top each serving with some pesto.

Prep Time: 15 Minutes

Cook Time: 50 Minutes

Servings: 4- 6

Ingredients

- 1 tbsp. olive oil
- 1 medium yellow onion, roughly chopped
- 2 tsp. curry powder
- 1 tsp. cumin seeds
- 1 c. dried lentils
- 1 14-oz. can diced tomatoes
- 1 13.5-oz. can coconut milk
- 1/4 tsp. red pepper flakes (optional)
- 1 c. whole milk yogurt
- 2 tsp. grated fresh ginger

Instructions

1. Heat the oil in a large saucepan or Dutch oven on medium. Add onion and cook, stirring occasionally, until tender (they should not brown), 5 to 7 minutes.

Stir in curry powder and cumin seeds and cook for 1 minute.

2. Stir in the lentils, then add 1/2 cup of water and the tomatoes (with their juices), coconut milk, red pepper flakes (if using), and 1 1/2 teaspoons salt. Bring to a simmer, then cover and gently simmer, stirring occasionally, until the lentils are tender, 35 to 45 minutes, adding water if it starts to look dry.

3. While the lentils cook, in a small bowl, combine yogurt, ginger and pinch salt.

4. Serve the lentils with a hefty dollop of the gingery yogurt. You could also serve this over rice or throw in some greens, such as spinach or arugula.

21. Thai Pineapple Shrimp Fried Rice

Prep Time: 15 Minutes

Cook Time: 50 Minutes

Servings: 4

Ingredients

- 3 tbsp. vegetable oil
- 1 lb. medium shrimp
- 1 large red bell pepper
- 1 medium Red Onion
- 2 clove garlic
- 1 red or green chile
- 2 large eggs
- 2 tbsp. fish sauce
- 2 tbsp. Soy Sauce
- 2 tbsp. lime juice
- 1 1/2 c. diced fresh pineapple
- 1/2 c. dry-roasted cashews
- 1/2 c. torn cilantro leaves

Instructions

1. Heat oil in a large nonstick skillet over medium-high heat; add shrimp and stir-fry 1 minute or until they turn pink on the outside but are only halfway cooked through. Remove shrimp to a plate with a slotted spoon.

2. Add to skillet bell pepper, onion, garlic, and chile; stir-fry 3 minutes or until onion is translucent. Add eggs and stir-fry 30 seconds.

3. Stir in 2 cups cooked rice, separating grains with back of spoon, and stir-fry 2 minutes. Add fish sauce, soy sauce, and lime juice; cook, stirring, for 2 minutes.

4. Return shrimp to skillet with fresh pineapple and stir-fry 2 minutes or until shrimp are cooked through.

5. Stir in cashews and cilantro.

Prep Time: 15 Minutes

Cook Time: 40 Minutes

Servings: 4

Ingredients

Yogurt Sauce

- 1 c. plain Greek yogurt
- c. chopped fresh mint
- 1/4 c. water
- 1/4 tsp. each ground cumin, garlic powder and salt
- meatballs
- c. plain dry bread crumbs
- 1 large egg
- c. water
- 1 tbsp. Dried Minced Onion
- 1 tsp. ground cumin
- 1/4 tsp. each garlic powder, salt and pepper
- 1 lb. Lean Ground Beef
- 1 lb. medium zucchini
- 1 medium Red Onion

- 2 tsp. olive oil
- 3 plum tomatoes
- Warmed pocketless pitas
- Lettuce (optional)

Instructions

1. Position racks to divide oven in thirds. Heat oven to 500°F. You'll need 2 rimmed baking pans lined with nonstick foil.
2. Mix all sauce ingredients in medium bowl, cover and refrigerate until ready to serve with meatballs.
3. Stir bread crumbs, egg, water, minced onion, cumin, garlic powder, salt and pepper until blended. Add beef; stir with fork until thoroughly blended. Roll rounded Tbsps into balls; place on a lined baking pan.
4. Put zucchini and red onion on other lined baking pan; toss with oil. Place vegetables on top rack, meatballs on bottom. Roast 20 minutes.
5. Remove pans from oven, turn browned vegetables over, then push to one side and add tomatoes; turn meatballs. Roast meatballs and vegetables 5 minutes more or until zucchini is tender; toss together.

6. Serve on pitas with lettuce if desired. Top with yogurt
    sauce.

Prep Time: 10 Minutes

Cook Time: 20 Minutes

Servings: 4

Ingredients

- 1 tbsp. extra-virgin olive oil
- 6 slice bacon or pancetta
- 1 1/2 c. Yukon gold or red-skinned potato
- 1 onion
- 8 large eggs
- 1/4 c. heavy cream
- 1/4 tsp. kosher salt
- 1/4 tsp. Freshly ground pepper
- 1/2 c. shredded Fontina cheese
- 2 tbsp. shredded Fontina cheese
- 1 tbsp. snipped fresh chives

Instructions

1. Heat broiler. Heat oil in a large nonstick skillet over medium heat. Add bacon and cook until fat is almost

rendered and bacon is starting to crisp; remove bacon to a paper towel to drain. Add potato and onion to drippings; raise heat to medium-high and sauté mixture until potato is almost tender, about 10 to 12 minutes.

2. Whisk eggs, cream, salt, and pepper in a medium bowl; stir in 1/2 cup of the cheese, then stir in bacon. Pour into skillet, shaking pan gently to distribute. Reduce heat to medium and cook, without stirring, 5 minutes, or until set on bottom and sides (eggs will be runny in center).

3. Place skillet under broiler; broil 2 minutes, or until frittata is firm in center. Sprinkle with the remaining 2 tablespoons cheese and chives. Loosen edges with a rubber spatula and slide onto a serving plate. Cut into wedges.

Prep Time: 10 Minutes

Cook Time: 20 Minutes

Servings: 4

Ingredients

- Salt
- 1 lb. nettle leaves
- 1/4 c. pine nuts, toasted
- 2 small cloves garlic, roughly chopped
- 1 tsp. grated lemon zest plus 3 Tbsp lemon juice
- 3 tbsp. extra virgin olive oil
- 4 oz. Parmesan, finely grated (about 1 cup), divided
- 1 lb. bucatini pasta (or spaghetti)
- 1 oz. fresh or frozen peas

Instructions

1. Prepare pesto: Bring large pot of salted water to a boil. Fill large bowl with ice water. Working in batches, plunge nettles into boiling water until wilted, 1 to 2 minutes. Immediately transfer to ice water, then drain

and squeeze mostly dry (you should have about 2 cups). Repeat with remaining nettles.

2. In food processor, pulse pine nuts and garlic until chopped. Add nettles, separating leaves, and pulse to chop, scraping down side. Add lemon zest and juice and oil and puree until nearly smooth. Add 1/2 cup Parmesan and 1/2 tsp salt and puree until creamy.

3. In second pot of water, cook pasta per package directions. Place peas in small strainer and dunk in boiling water 1 minute before pasta is done; drain peas. Reserve 1 cup cooking water; drain pasta and return it to pot. Toss with 3/4 cup pesto and 1/4 cup Parmesan, adding reserved water until pasta is well coated. Fold in peas; serve with remaining Parmesan.

Prep Time: 15 Minutes

Cook Time: 45 Minutes

Servings: 4

Ingredients

- 1/4 c. olive oil
- 2 tbsp. fresh lemon juice
- 2 small pepperoncini
- 1 medium shallot
- 1 tbsp. red wine vinegar
- 1/2 tsp. lemon zest
- 1 1/4 tsp. salt
- 2 c. fresh lima and cranberry beans
- 1/2 c. small mint leaves
- 8 oz. halloumi cheese
- Freshly ground pepper

Instructions

1. In a medium bowl, whisk together oil, juice, pepperoncini, shallot, vinegar, and zest. Set vinaigrette aside.

2. In a medium pot over high heat, bring 3 cups salted water and beans to a boil. Reduce heat to low, simmering until tender, 15 to 20 minutes. Drain beans and rinse under cold water. Toss beans, parsley, and mint with reserved vinaigrette to combine.

3. Cut cheese into 1/4-inch-thick slices. In a skillet over medium-high heat, sear cheese until golden brown, about 4 minutes per side.

4. To serve, divide bean salad and cheese among four plates, and season with pepper to taste.

Prep Time: 15 Minutes

Cook Time: 45 Minutes

Servings: 12

Ingredients

- 1 lb. red or Yukon Gold potatoes
- 1 package elbow macaroni
- 1 1/2 c. mayonnaise
- 3 celery ribs
- 2 peeled and grated
- 2 hard-boiled eggs
- 1/2 lb. ham
- 1/2 c. frozen peas
- 1/2 c. chopped dill pickles
- 1/4 c. finely chopped red onion
- 2 tsp. seasoned salt (I like Lawry's)
- 1/2 tsp. Freshly ground black pepper

Instructions

1. Bring 2 large saucepans of salted water to a boil.

2. Cut the potatoes into 1-inch cubes. Add them to one pot of boiling water and simmer until fork- tender, about 8 minutes. Drain well and set aside.

3. Cook the elbow macaroni in the second saucepan of boiling water until al dente, according to the directions on the package. Drain well, and set aside.

4. Transfer the potatoes and pasta to a large salad bowl. Add all the remaining ingredients and toss well. Add more seasoned salt and black pepper if necessary. Cover, and refrigerate the salad until ready to serve.

Prep Time: 15 Minutes

Cook Time: 30 Minutes

Servings: 4

Ingredients

- 1 lb. (21- to 25-count) peeled and deveined shrimp
- 1 lb. asparagus, trimmed and cut into 2-in. pieces
- 2 medium leeks, white and light green parts only, cut into 3/4-in.-thick rounds
- 2 tbsp. olive oil
- Kosher salt and pepper
- 2 lemons, halved
- 1/2 c. mayonnaise
- 1 1/2 tbsp. harissa paste

Instructions

1. Heat grill to medium-high. Thread shrimp, asparagus and leek rounds onto skewers. Brush lightly with oil and season with 1/2 tsp. each salt and pepper.

2. Grill skewers until vegetables are tender and shrimp are opaque throughout, 3 to 4 minutes per side.

3. Place lemons on grill alongside skewers, cut sides down, and grill until charred, about 4 minutes.

4. Into small bowl, squeeze 2 tsp. juice from 1 charred lemon half. Stir in mayonnaise and harissa to combine. Serve skewers with harissa mayo and remaining charred lemon halves.

Prep Time: 15 Minutes

Cook Time: 25 Minutes

Servings: 4

Ingredients

- 2 oz. spaghetti
- 1 lemon
- 2 tbsp. olive oil
- 2 cloves garlic, finely chopped
- 1 lb. Lean Ground Beef
- Kosher salt and pepper
- 2 tbsp. tomato paste
- 1/2 c. dry white wine
- 1 pt. cherry or grape tomatoes, halved
- 1/4 red onion, thinly sliced
- Grated Parmesan and small fresh basil leaves, for serving

Instructions

1. Cook the pasta according to package directions. Reserve 1 cup cooking liquid, drain.

2. Grate the zest of the lemon directly into the pot, then squeeze in the juice (you should have about 2 teaspoons zest and 3 tablespoons juice). Drizzle with 1 tablespoon oil and toss to combine (adding some of the reserved cooking liquid if the pasta seems dry).

3. While the pasta is cooking, heat the remaining tablespoon oil in a large skillet over medium-high heat. Add the garlic and cook, stirring, until it starts to brown around the edges, about 1 minute. Add the beef, season with 1/2 teaspoon each salt and pepper and cook, breaking it up with a spoon until browned, 4 to 6 minutes.

4. Add the tomato paste and cook, stirring, until the beef starts to get a bit crispy. Add the wine and simmer until it evaporates, 2 to 3 minutes. Toss the beef with the pasta and top with the tomatoes and onion. Sprinkle with Parmesan and basil, if desired.

Prep Time: 20 Minutes

Cook Time: 10 Minutes

Servings: 20

Ingredients

Shrimp Boil:

- 16 c. water
- 1/4 c. sugar
- 1 tbsp. kosher salt
- 2 tbsp. Creole spice
- 1/4 c. lemon juice
- 4 bay leaves
- 1 tbsp. coriander seeds
- 1 tbsp. black peppercorns
- 2 large sprigs thyme
- 1 onion
- 1 head garlic
- 32 large shrimp

Remoulade:

- 3/4 c. mayonnaise

- 1/4 c. Dijon mustard
- 1 shallot
- 2 tbsp. Creole spice
- 2 tbsp. white wine vinegar
- 1 1/2 tbsp. prepared horseradish
- 1 tsp. lemon juice
- 1/2 tsp. minced garlic
- 1/2 tsp. paprika
- 1/2 tsp. hot-red-pepper sauce
- 1/4 tsp. celery salt
- 8 c. mixed baby greens (such as Lolla Rossa lettuce, green and red oak leaf lettuce, tatsoi, or mizuna)

Instructions

1. To make shrimp boil: In a large pot, bring all ingredients except shrimp to a boil; add shrimp and cook 4 minutes, or until just cooked through. Drain; lay out shrimp on a baking sheet and refrigerate to cool.

2. To make rémoulade: Pulse all ingredients except greens in a food processor until just blended. Transfer mixture to a large bowl; add shrimp and toss. Refrigerate at least 1 hour or up to 8.

3. To serve, mound salad greens on each.

Prep Time: 20 Minutes

Cook Time: 20 Minutes

Servings: 4

Ingredients

- 1 c. long-grain white rice
- 1 tsp. grated orange zest
- 8 small chicken thighs (about 2 1/4 lbs)
- 2 tsp. olive oil
- Kosher salt
- Pepper
- 1 clove garlic, finely chopped
- 1 (1-inch) piece ginger, finely chopped
- 1/3 c. orange juice
- 1 pt. grape tomatoes
- 1/4 c. cilantro leaves, finely chopped

Instructions

1. Heat oven to 425°F. Cook rice per package directions. Fluff with a fork and fold in orange zest.

2. Meanwhile, heat a large skillet on medium. Rub chicken with oil, then season with ½ tsp each salt and pepper. Place chicken in the skillet skin side down and cook until golden brown and crisp, 10 to 12 minutes. Flip and cook 1 minute more; transfer to plate.

3. Add garlic and ginger to skillet and cook, stirring, 1 minute. Add orange juice and cook, scraping bottom of skillet, for 1 minute. Add tomatoes and cook, tossing occasionally, for 3 minutes. Nestle chicken into tomato mixture, transfer skillet to oven, and roast until cooked through, 5 to 6 minutes. Serve over orange rice and top with cilantro.